Copyright © 2022.
Written by Kristy Winter

Illustrated by Kristy Winter, Stephan Lueke, and Yue Conway.
Yellow blossoms blooming through generations.

Table of Contents

Master shrinkers and growers.
How can we help you today? Call 1-800-686-000 today.
Cockroach plumber. We clean and repair all your pipes.
Kristy Winter 2022.

Cockroach Plumber Company.

Are you having trouble getting those hairballs out of your pipes?

Well, we are here to help.

Do you have leaky or broken pipes?

Let us help you.

We are not your normal plumbers. We can shrink and go inside your pipes and find out what's really going on. We can find any lost items that fall down your pipes.

We are the plumber cockroaches which you will find nowhere else. We grow and shrink to clean and repair all your pipes.

Just give us a call at 1-800-686-000 and we will be there in a flash.

Banging Pipes.

"Yes, hello. My name is Daphnia Drum. I have a problem with my kitchen pipes under the sink. They keep making a loud banging and screeching noise. Can you send someone over right away?"

Hello,
Yes. I need
a cockroach
plumber for
my banging
screeching
pipes.
I need
a good
plumber.
Kristy Winter 2022.

"Yes, ma'am. We have a cockroach plumber who is specialized in banging pipes. He will be right over."

Yes, maam we will send a plumber your way.
Cockroach Plumber Company
We fix all your pipes.
Just give us a call 1-800-686-000.
Kristy Winter 2022.

"Oh, thank you so much."

"You're welcome, ma'am."

Knock, knock, knock.

"I'll be right there!"

Daphnia opens the door and sees the cockroach plumber.

"Wow, you were so quick in getting here. Thank you so much. Let me show you the pipes under the sink."

The cockroach plumber follows her to check the pipes.

"Oh, I see. I know exactly what to do. I will come to get you when I am done."

"Thank you so much."

The cockroach plumber got right to work. He knew exactly who and what were in those pipes. He shrank down to the perfect size and crawled in the pipe.

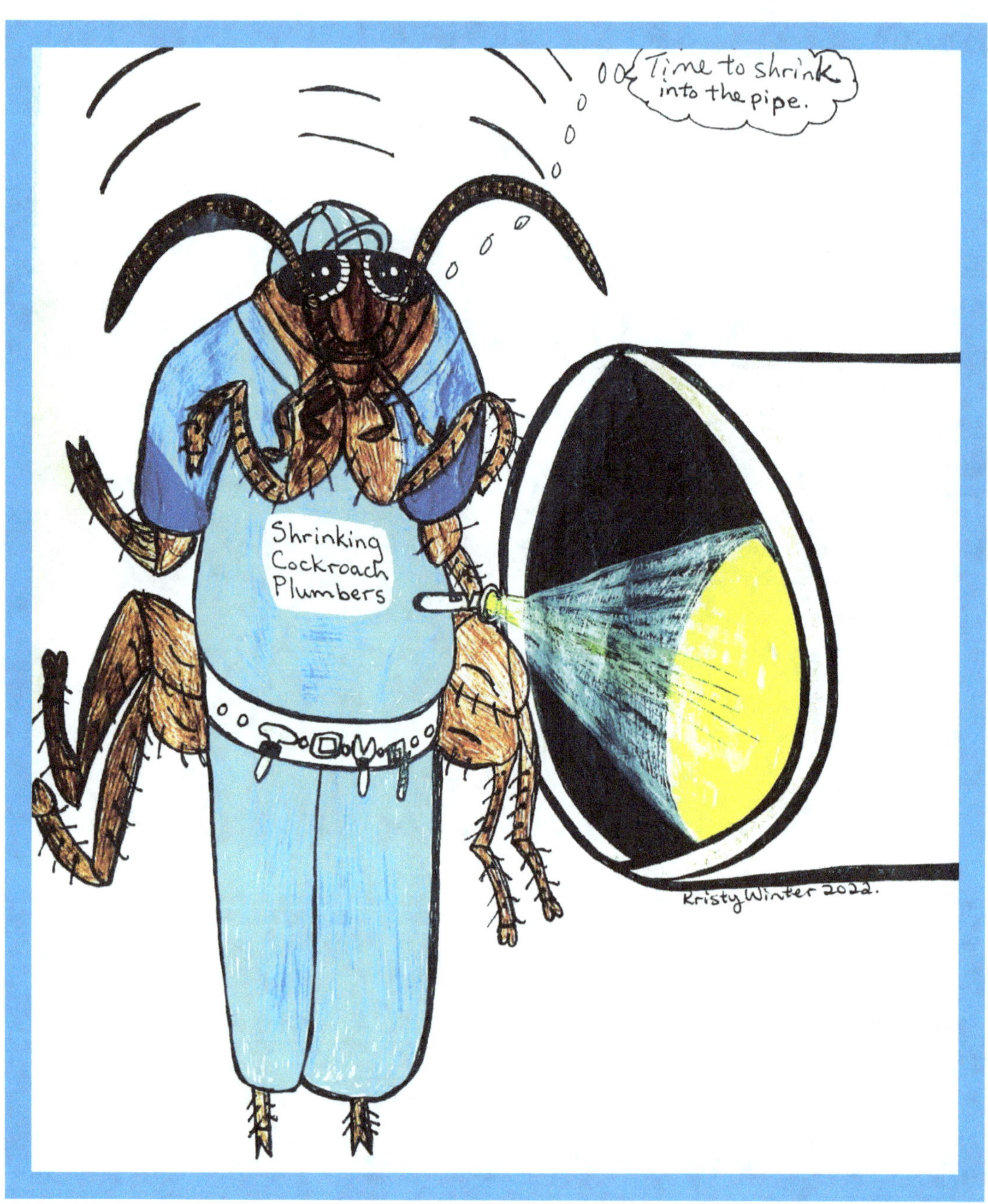
Time to shrink into the pipe.
Shrinking Cockroach Plumbers
Kristy Winter 2022.

"I thought so, just as I suspected. Water fleas. Hey, guys. Sorry to interrupt your band practice, but I am going to have to ask you to come with me."

Eee ya woo ha yeah!
Sorry But you'll have to come with me.
Banging Screeching Flea Band
Kristy Winter 2021
All the banging noise you can handle. The Fleas.
zzz

"We can't. We just got here. Yeah, and the acoustic sound is perfect in here. The drum beat holds so well too."

"Hey, if you come with me, I can get you a bigger pipe and have a sound proof room, so you can play as loud as you want whenever you want. I also, can send you some fans to hear you play. What do ya say?"

"Well, alright, but it better be awesome or we are coming back here."

"Ok, thank you so much. Just follow me out and then you can put your microphone, guitar, and drums in a special van I have just for you. You'll have to ride in my pocket until I get you outside and then you can follow me to the special place. There are other water fleas there too if you want any advise, or if you want to jam with them."

"Sounds great!"

The water fleas grabbed their instruments and followed the cockroach out of the pipes. The cockroach grew back to human size and gave the water fleas the special van they could put their instruments in and they could ride in.

"Wow, our instruments fit perfectly in here."

"Alright, I'm going to put you in my pocket now."

"Ok, thank you for the warning."

He placed them in his pocket and proceeded to find Daphnia.

"All is fixed and there will be no more noises, ma'am."

Wow, thank you so much. Here is a special tip for your great work and coming so quickly."

"You're welcome. Have a good day."

"You too."

The cockroach plumber left the house and walked around the block and took out the flea van.

"Alright, here is the pipe I was telling you about. All you have to do is drive down to pipe number 3A and that is your spot Feel free to knock on doors 4, 5, 6, and 7. If this works for you, call me at 1-800-686-000 and ask for Harold. Then I will send some more fans to hear you play."

"Thanks so much. I'm sure we will. Take care."

Upstream Trio
Playing in Pipe 3A tonight!
9pm to 2am!
Eel ya woo na yeah!
Banging and screeching Flea band.
Water Flea Band: all the banging you can handle.
Kristy Winter 2023.

The Hair Clog.

"Hello, yes, I have a really bad hair clog in my tub drain. I've tried to pull it all out. I just can't get it, it won't budge. Could you please send someone as soon as you can?"

"Yes, ma'am. How did the hair get clogged in there?"

"I was washing my dog and it normally goes right down the drain, but this time it got clogged. Not only that, but it seems as though the hair is growing out of the pipe drain like a plant."

"Alright, ma'am. We will send someone right over."

"Thank you so much."

"I better call Cteno Cephalides for this job it sounds serious."

Knock, knock, knock. The woman opened the door and showed the cockroach plumber the tub drain.

Kristy Winter 2020.
Entrance to Flea Hair Salon
Flea Circus Entrance

"I will get on this right away. This will definitely grow more if I don't take care of it immediately. I'll come get you when I am done."

"Oh, thank you so much!"

"You're welcome, ma'am."

"Ok, assistant Cteno Cephalides, you know what to do."

"Yes. I will investigate for fleas in the hair pipe."

"Good luck."

"No problem."

The assistant crawled down the Canis hairs into the pipe. First he found a circus with a tent of hair and all sorts of acts.

Georgia and Frank Forever
Kristy Winter 2008
Ta da!
I can hang
upside down
on a ring!

Flea Acrobats at 9:00p.m.! Tonight!
We balance each other out!

Our balance makes us one unit.
Flea Approved. Bite Proof.
Canine Dental Floss. The strongest in the world.
Kristy Winter 2022.

Flea Clown Act
At 2:00pm.

"Alright, guys I am going to have to ask you to leave this pipe."

"But, why? We have so many flea customers and flea acts."

"Tell you what. I have a special dog hair dome just for you. It holds all your tents, wires, and everything you'll need. I also, have a lot of flea friends who I would invite to come see your acts. You just have to come with me out of this pipe."

"Ok, but if you're lying we'll come right back here."

"Alright, follow me and get into my large assistants pocket and he will take you to the spot."

"Ok, but don't forget to go down a little farther down the pipe to get our cousins the pulex irritans."

"Ok, here you go. Here's my assistant."

"Hello, nice to meet all of you. I will be your ride to the hair dome."

"Ok, but we are waiting on our cousins before we go."

"Ok."

"I'll be right back with your cousins."

"Thanks."

Cteno Cephalides crawled back into the thick canis hair pipe.

"I don't see anyone yet."

He then heard some high pitched singing.

"We do hair. We connect it, to other fleas heads. They like it and we shape it."

Then he saw the pulex irritans.

"Hello, there. Sorry to interrupt your singing, but I have to ask all of you to take your hair and come with me."

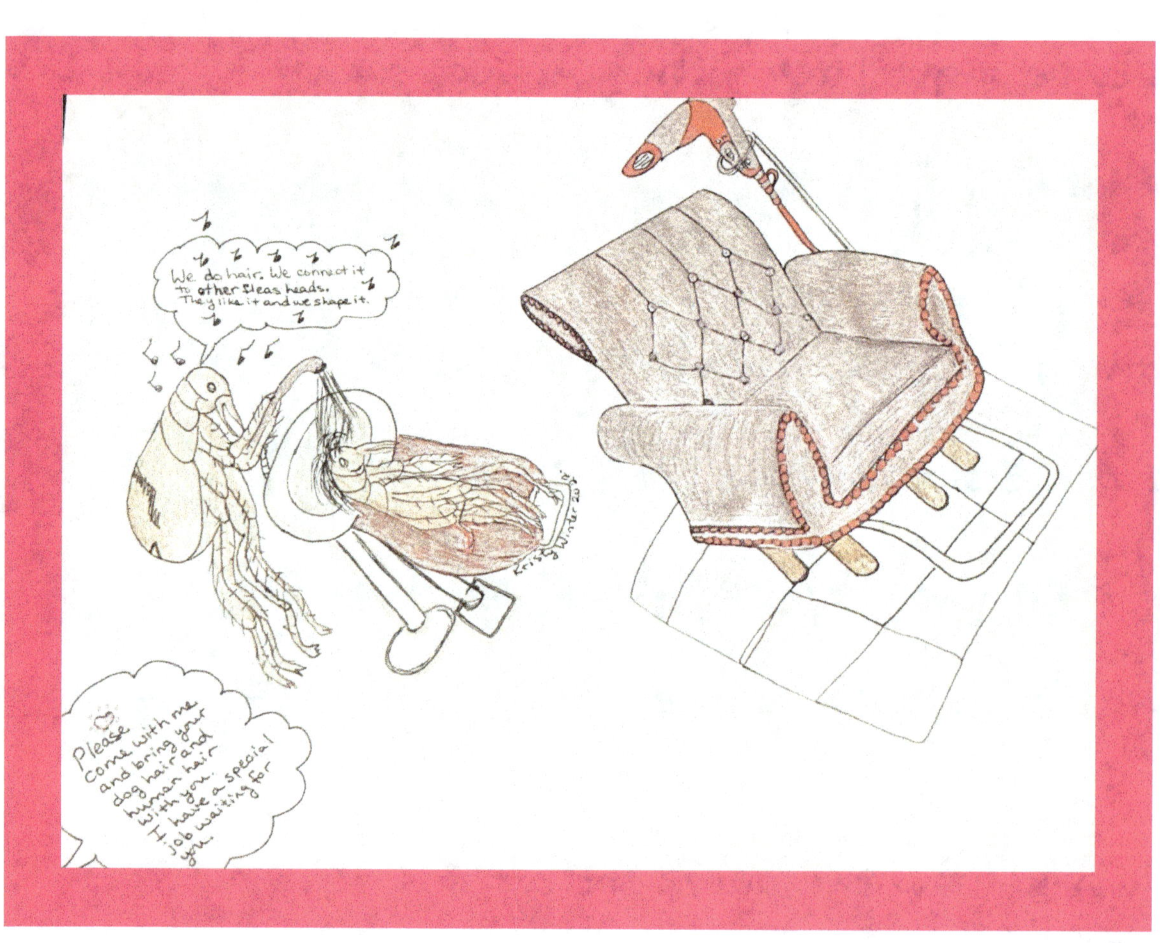

We do hair. We connect it to other fleas heads. They like it and we shape it.
Please come with me and bring your dog hair and human hair with you. I have a special job waiting for you.

"Why do we need to go with you?"

"I have some special humans who would love for you to help their hair look fabulous by doing hair replacements on their heads. They are in great need of your services."

"Really. Could we style their hair as well?"

"Of course. I can also send you many clients and advertise your hair salon for you. If it works out for you, I will help you grow into a great business with the humans."

"Ok, it's a deal!"

The pulex irritans grabbed all their canis hair out of the pipe along with some human hair and left the pipe.

"Just get into my assistants pocket and he will take you to your new business area."

"Ok."

"Hello, welcome. Come with me, please."

"Hey, cousins. So, good to see you're coming too!"

"Yeah, they offered us a hair salon with the humans."

"Wow! We are going to have a flea circus in a dog hair dome with everything we need or want."

"Cool!"

"Yeah!"

"Alright, Ctenos Cephalides, we have to go now. We can't have the human see you're a flea in her tub. She'll freak."

"I'm coming."

"Alright, all clear in the pipe, ma'am. You should have no more dog hair problems."

"Oh, thank you! Thank you!"

"I would put a hair collector over your drain next time you wash your dog in the tub, though."

"I will. Thank you so much."

"Alright, all is clear. Here is your dog hair dome and all the supplies."

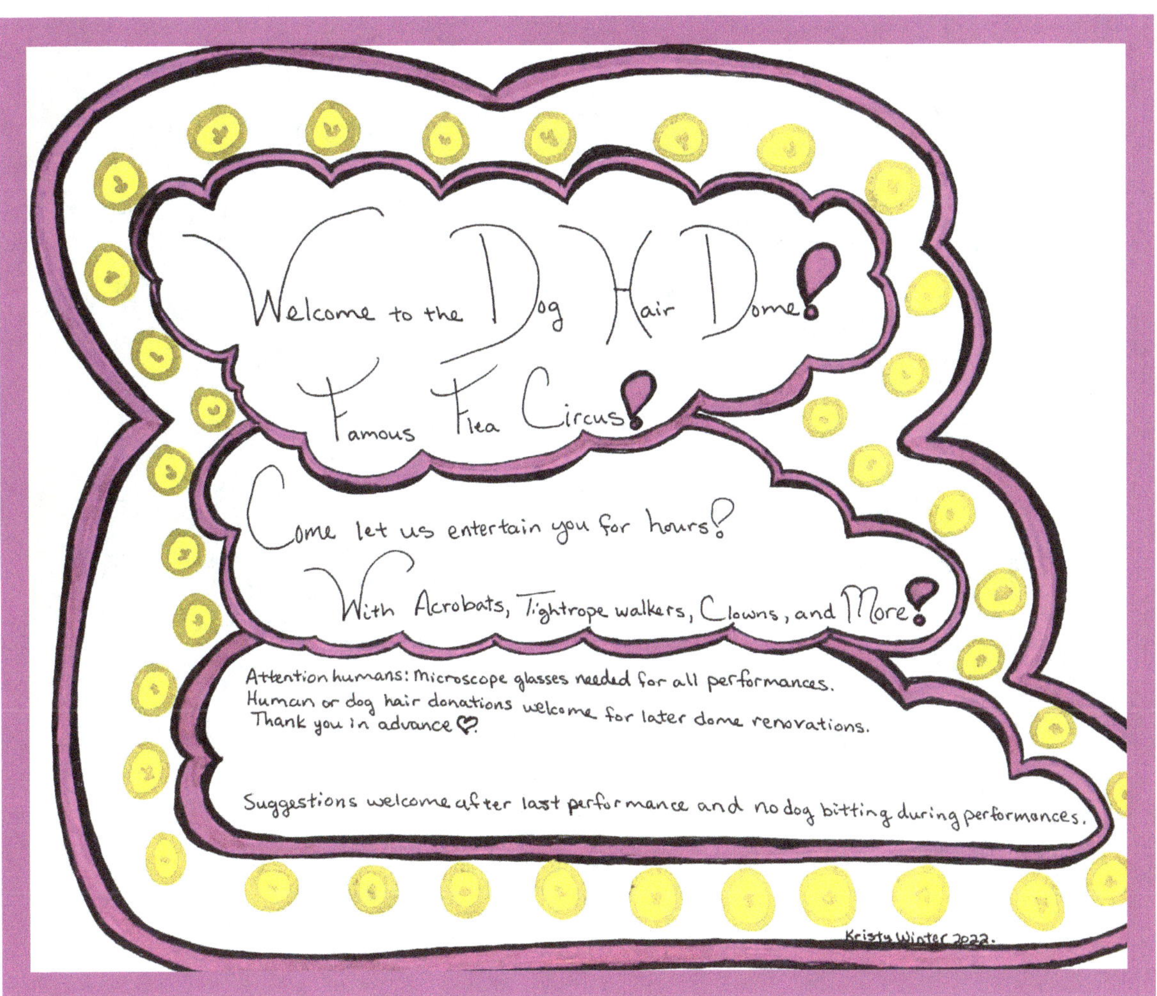

Welcome to the Dog Hair Dome!
Famous Flea Circus!
Come let us entertain you for hours!
With Acrobats, Tightrope walkers, Clowns, and More!
Attention humans: microscope glasses needed for all performances.
Human or dog hair donations welcome for later dome renovations.
Thank you in advance.
Suggestions welcome after last performance and no dog bitting during performances.
Kristy Winter 2022.

Welcome to the dog Hair Dome!
For Fleas and humans with microscopes
Famous Flea Circus
Flea Circus
Tickets
Cash
Trade hair for cash
Cash
Tickets
Trade hair for cash
I'd like two waters please.
Kristy Winter 2020
Yes, please!
OK.
We want cotton candy.

"Thank you so much! It is wonderful here!"

"Call me at 1-800-686-000 if you need anything and ask for George."

"Will do. Thanks again."

"You're welcome."

"See ya cousins. Call us so we can come see your salon."

"We will."

"Alright, now over here are your humans who have been waiting for you to help them."

"Wow! So many clients!"

"This is. Lisa Lice, she will be helping you call the human clients."

"Nice to meet you, purlex irritans, we have been hoping for someone like you to work with our hair follicles. The last purlex irritans only wanted to live in our clients hair."

"No, ma'am, we love to groom, style, and grow hair by using clean dog hair extensions."

"Oh, how wonderful. Let's get started."

"Yes, let's get to work!"

"Amazing, I thought I would never look like this again! Thank you so much!"

"You're welcome. Next."

Human and Flea Connection Hair Salon.
Are you missing patches of hair that just won't grow back or won't stay on?
Well, we are here to help those lazy Follicles wake up and get back on track!
Just give us a call at
1-800-332-003
for an appointment to get you back on track?
Kristy Winter 2022.

Welcome to
Human and Flea Connection
Hair Salon.
The growth that connects us all.
• Hair imptants that naturally grow your own hair.
• Washes & styles and much more.
• Walkins welcome or come on in and make an appointment.
Kristy Winter 2022.

Plumber Alert.

"Hello. Yes, I'm calling in regards to your plumbing services, but will need the special cockroach plumber. We have had termites that have chewed up our pipes. Please send him quickly."

"Yes, ma'am. What's your address?"

"2013 Cryptotermes Brevis Lane Termite, Kansas 66512."

"We will send him immediately to you."

"Thank you so much and please hurry!"

The special cockroach plumber arrives with his assistant. The plumber knocks on the door and the woman opens the door.

"Oh, thank you so much for coming so quickly. Let me show you where they have been."

The special cockroach plumber and his assistant follow the woman. She proceeds to the bathroom and opens the door.

"As you can see they have been busy. I did not think they would eat the pipes, but apparently these termites love my pipes."

A bunch of termites scurry down the broken pipe.

"Alright assistant, you know what to do. Ma'am, we will take it from here."

"Thank you so much."

"Yes, no problem. We will have them gone within the hour and your pipes back to normal."

"Ok! I'll leave you two to it."

(I wanted to interject for a moment in the story and thank Stephan Lueke a.k.a. Mr. Blue Sky for this wonderful painting he did for me.)

The assistant quickly jumps into the pipes and finds all of the termites gathered in a joint in the pipe. The assistant quickly does a jump side kick and knocks all of the termites out.

Knock out time! Side kick!
Oh no! Not you!
Kristy Winter 2022.

The assistant taps on the pipes alerting the special cockroach plumber the job is done. The special cockroach plumber taps once on the pipe to signal he is ready. The assistant lines up all the termites and side kicks them out of the broken part of the pipe. The special cockroach turns on the water and flushes out the rest of the termite nest and gathers them all up. The assistant rubs its feet together and seals the hole as the special cockroach plumber adds a special tubing to secure the hole. Then the plumber adds a home remedy glue to the outer covering. He picks up all the termites that are knocked out and puts them in his pocket.

"Problem solved ma'am. Please wait 24 hours for the glue to dry. Would you like to recycle your termites or have them put to work?"

"Recycle them, please. Thank you so much. Here is a tip for your speedy services."

"Thank you ma'am! Alright we're off."

The termites get put in a special training camp to work on fixing broken pipes and are rewarded with as many wood chips as they desire so they won't want to eat pipes and get upset stomachs.

The Giant Leak.

"Hello? Hello? Is anybody there?"

"Yes, ma'am. Calm down we are here to help. What seems to be the matter ma'am?"

"I have a huge leak coming from my basement pipes. I tried to turn the water off in the house, but it won't stop coming out."

"We will send the emergency team right away ma'am. Now where are you located?"

"I live at 353 Springtail Lane Achorutes, Kansas 62583.

Please hurry, it's starting to snow and I don't want my pipes to freeze."

"They are ten minutes away ma'am."

"Thank you so much."

The cockroach plumber arrives at Spring Snowflake's house and knocks on the door.

Mrs. Snowflake whips the door open and grabs the cockroach plumber by the shirt and practically flies down the stairs.

"Here is the leak. I'm sorry to rush you, but I just don't want it to freeze!"

"Yes, Mrs. Snowflake we will take care of it immediately. We will come get you when it is fixed."

"Ok, thank you so much!"

"Alright, Nivicola team, get to work blocking those holes."

"Yes, sir! "

Five springtails jump out of the cockroach plumber's pocket and spring towards the leaking pipe.

OK, team
let's get to
work!
Kristy Winter 2022.

The cockroach plumber shrinks to the exact size
of the pipe and crawls into the pipe.

Time to shrink into the pipe.
Shrinking Cockroach Plumbers
Kristy Winter 2022.

"Alright, where are you springtails? I know you're practicing in here. Awe, there you are."

The cockroach plumber sees ten springtails doing floor routines on the pipe and breaking the pipe with every landing.

The Spring Dropping Floor Routine.
We love doing our floor routines in these pipes. Get ready to spring into action.
Kristy Winter 2022.

"Excuse me fine gymnasts, but could you stop for just a moment so I can talk to you?"

"Yes, what is it you need cockroach?"

"I am looking for a gymnastic team like yours to get some old rusted sprinklers to work again. Do you think you can help me?"

The springtails discussed the idea and replied, "What's in it for us?"

"All I need for you to do is clean these sprinklers by puncturing them with your fantastic moves, so we can water these lawns. If you do this for me, I will see that your floor routines will be seen by the famous Spring Nivicola team. What do you say?"

"Hmm. Alright, but we want to see the team first."

"No problem, just come with me. They are fixing the pipe outside as we speak."

"What! They are here!"

"Yes, they work with me as a side job to practice there jumping and flying skills."

The springtails go with the cockroach and crawl out of the pipe. The cockroach plumber grows back to normal size and finishes sealing the last hole. The Spring Nivicola team greets the gymnasts team.

"Hello, very nice to meet you. You have some very nice work here for us to repair. We even had to invent a new routine to patch your holes. Thank you so much."

"No, no. It is very nice to meet you, Nivicola team. We are eager to learn from you after the work we are going to perform for the cockroach. Where did he go by the way?"

"Oh, he's a lot taller now, so you'll have to look behind and up to see him."

The springtails turned around and looked up.

"Gulp. Wow! You're really big now!"

"Yes, I am a special cockroach. We help the humans fix their pipe problems and give insects and others in need, like you a job that they love and will be appreciated for. The growing and shrinking is a perk of the job."

"Wow! Sounds fun. Do you ever scare the humans when you show up at their door?"

"At first they were scared, but they really liked our work and got used to us. We were more efficient than the humans and they liked that."

"Ok. Where do we go?"

"First, get into my pocket so the human doesn't see you."

"Ok!"

"Mrs. Snowflake, your pipes are fixed and will not freeze now."

"Oh, thank you so much. Please have some hot chocolate with marshmallows to warm you up before you leave."

"Thank you, ma'am. Have a good day."

"Ok, springtails. All is clear and here are your sprinklers to clean."

The springtails cleaned all the sprinklers and placed perfect holes in each one. Then the Spring Nivicola team worked with the springtails to learn their new routine and became part of the Spring Nivicola team.

The Job Recruiter

"Hello, Yes. I am calling in regards to some rhinoceros beetles. They are in my bathroom and I can't get rid of them. I know you are not exterminators. I have read your ad and was wondering if you had any job openings for them?"

"Yes, ma'am. We do not exterminate any insect no matter what it is and usually we fix leaks and clogs. For your special case we need to know what they are doing and where in your bathroom they are located."

"Ok, yes. Well, they are all over my toilet and frankly, I can't go to the bathroom or relax in the tub due to their motorcycle vrooming all about here and there."

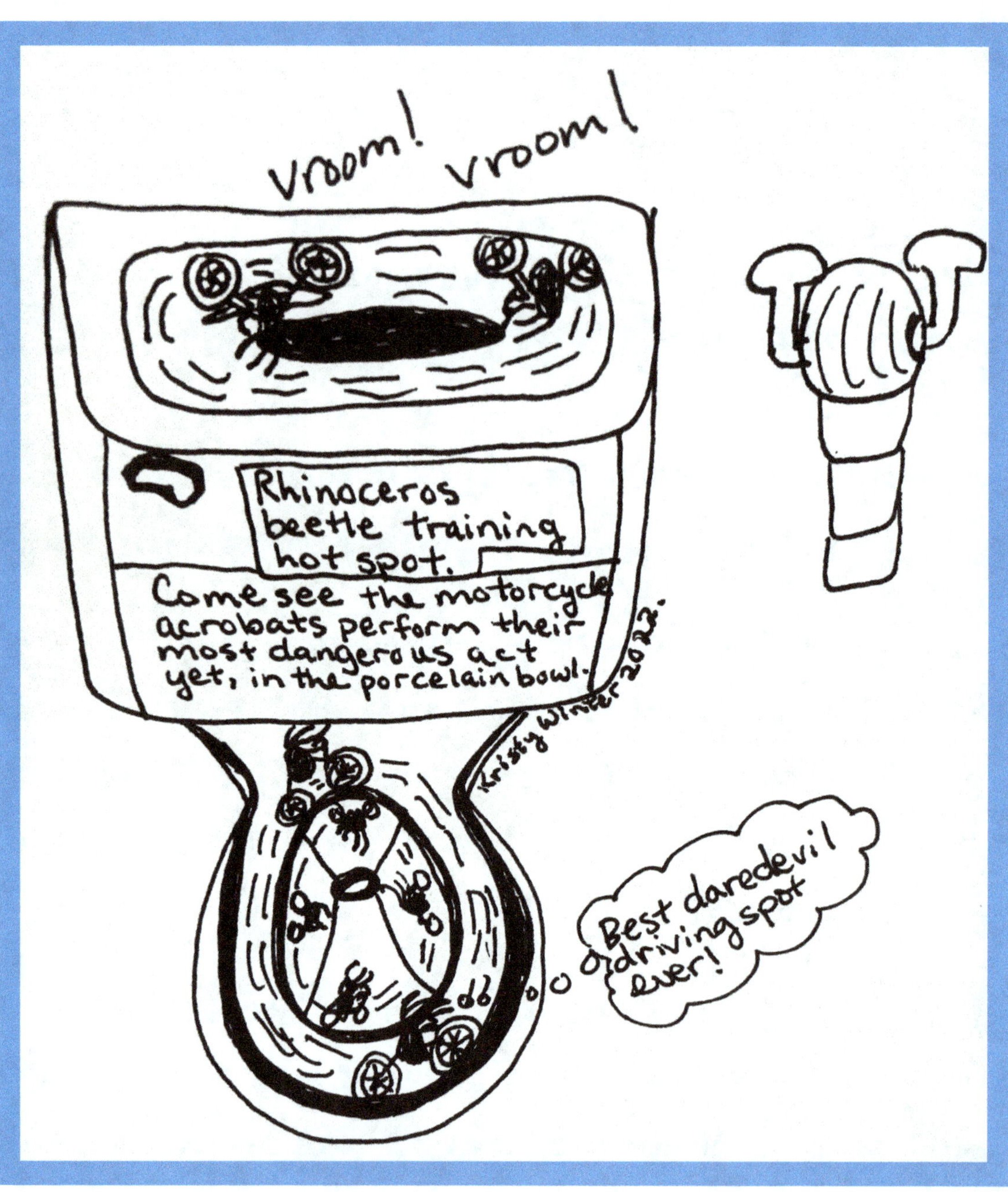

vroom! vroom!
Rhinoceros beetle training hot spot.
Come see the motorcycle acrobats perform their most dangerous act yet, in the porcelain bowl.
Kristy Winter 2022
Best daredevil driving spot ever!

Ready to ride the porcelain circles. Yeah!

"Ok. I think we can find them a job. Let me talk to my boss and I'll get back with you shortly, if that's ok?"

"Oh, yes, please and thank you. I have been using my neighbors bathroom. They've been so kind so far, but I don't know how much longer they'll have me."

"Yes, ma'am. I will get back to you as soon as I can."

"Thank you so much, goodbye. Oh my number is 816-222-3333, when you are ready with an answer."

"Ok. We'll give you a call."

"Sinodendron Cylindricum, we have some rhinoceros beetles that might need a job. They drive motorcycles in the porcelain bowl. Do you think you can use them?"

"I'll have to go talk to the rhinoceros beetles first and see if they want the job I'm thinking of. Call the lady back and tell her I'll be over for an interview with her beetles. Also, tell her not to talk to the beetles just yet."

"Ok, Sinodendron. I'll let her know."

"Miss, my boss wants to come and interview your beetles, but he doesn't want you to talk to them just yet. Do you think you can do that?"

"Oh, yes. As long as he can get them to go somewhere away from my house and bathroom."

"What's your name and address, please?"

"My name is Bee Beetle. I live at 2020 Vroom Vroom Lane Rhino, Kansas 33321."

"I will let him know. His name is Sinodendron and he said he will be there in about 20 minutes, if that works for you?"

"Oh, yes. That's fine. Thank you so much."

Knock, knock, knock.

"Oh, that must be him."

She opens the door and sees a giant rhinoceros beetle.

"Are yyyou Sinodendron?"

"Yes, ma'am. Sorry to startle you. I know you were expecting a cockroach, but this is a special job that I do for the company when needed."

Are yyyou
Sinodendron?
Hello, maam.
Sorry to
startle you.
Yes.
Special Insect Job Recruiter
Kristy Winter 2022.

"Oh, yes. They are in here and I didn't tell them anything."

"Thank you. It's better they aren't expecting me. They get irritated easily."

"Oh."

"Please wait in another room and I will let you know how it goes and if I want to hire them."

"Ok. Thank you."

"You're welcome."

The giant rhinoceros beetle proceeds into the bathroom very slowly and quietly opens the door and closes it gently.

Vroom, vroom, vroom.

"Hello, my dear daredevil drivers. The human was wondering if you would like to work for me. What do you think? I have a special tub that you can drive in that changes into ramps and steps."

"Hmm. Interesting proposition. What's in it for us?"

"Well, you can be as loud as you like and I will bring some other beetles to watch you if you like. I can pay you in whatever form of payment you like and you can have the place for free."

"Hmm. Will there be any bowls like this one near the tub?"

"Oh, yes. You can switch back and forth between the two. I just ask that you park your motorcycles for 10 minutes at 1pm everyday so we can refill your motorcycles with special gas."

"Hmm. What does the gas do?"

"It helps you to go faster and for longer periods of time. Regular gas will only last you about 5hrs. Our gas will last you until 1pm the next day. We would also like to tune your motorcycles as well so they can drive this long with no issues. What do you say?"

"Ok. Where do we go?"

"I will take you one block down and let you try it out and you tell me what you think. If you like it I have a special trainer as well to show you some new tricks you can do to excite your audience."

"Ok. Sounds good we're in."

"Please take your motorcycles and put them in this special box."

"Ok."

The giant rhino beetle picks up the other beetles and their motorcycles. Then tells the woman that he has hired the rhinoceros beetles and she is good to go to the bathroom.

"Oh, thank you so much! I hope they enjoy their new job."

"You're welcome, ma'am."

Sinodendron takes them to the special job and they love it. They get lots of beetles to watch their daredevil stunts and they become very famous.

The Clogged Toilet.

"Yes, hello. Can you send someone to unclog my toilet. No matter what I do with the plunger it won't come out."

"Yes, ma'am. We have just the right cockroach for the job. We will send him right over."

"Thank you so much!"

"You're welcome, ma'am."

"By the way where do you live?"

"I live at Dung Beetle Lane Sculpture, Kansas 33210."

"Thank you. He'll be right over."

"Scarabaeus Viettei, they are doing it again. Can you take this job?"

"Yes, I'll see which spot I can transport them to."

The cockroach plumber arrives at the woman's door and she takes him to the toilet.

"I see. I will get right on it, ma'am. This might take awhile and it will be very smelly and messy. You might want to stay somewhere with the windows open."

"Ok. Let me know when you have unclogged it. I will wait in here."

"Alright. The coast is clear. Scarabaeus get to work."

"Yes."

He crawls out of the plumber's pocket and into the toilet.

As he crawls in he sees multiple sculptures blocking the entrance. He knocks on the wall door opening.

"Yes, how can I help you? I am very busy making my sculptures."

"Sorry to bother you sir. By the way I love your fecal sculptures. I am in need of an artist like you for my gallery. Are you interested?"

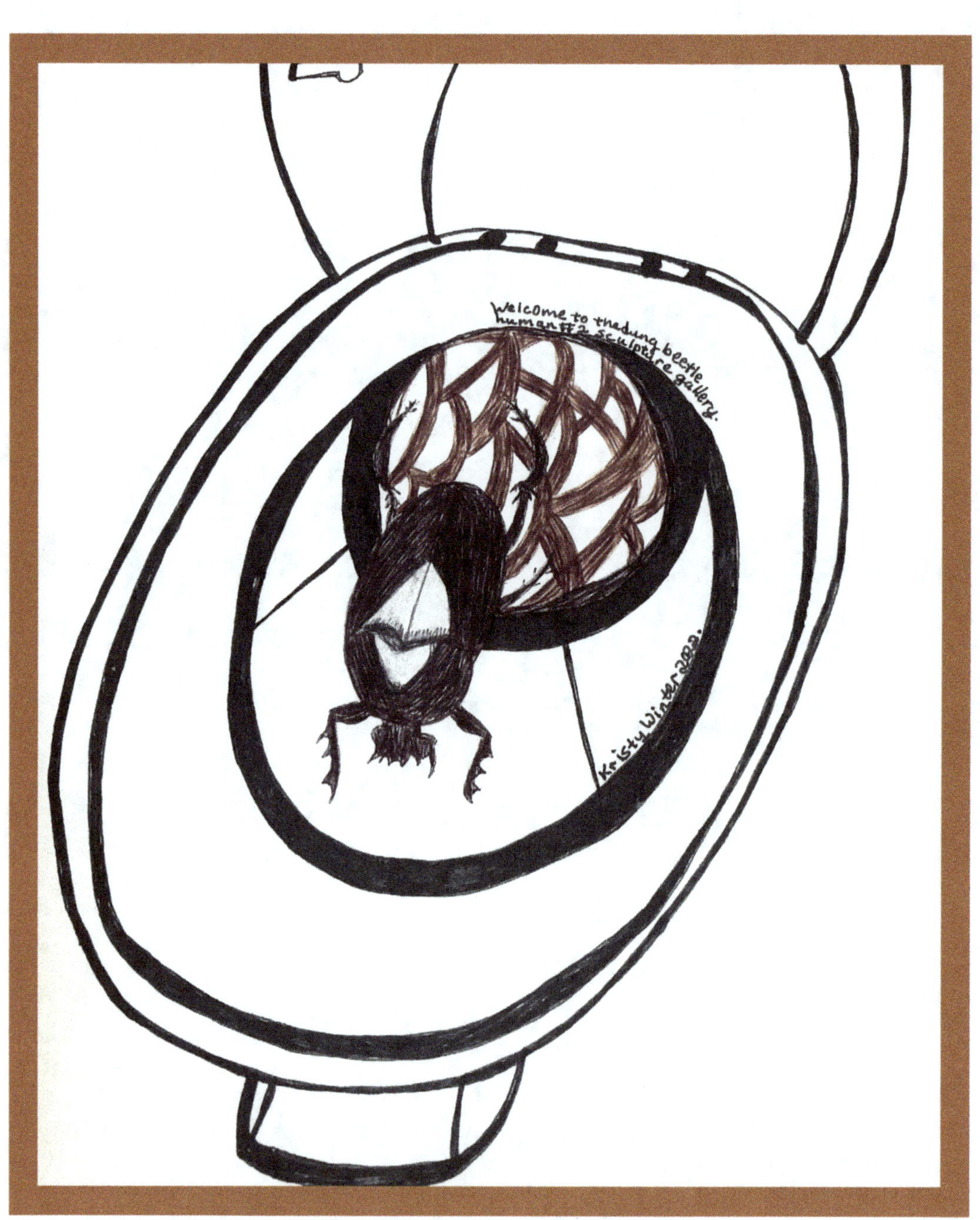

Welcome to the dung beetle human #2 sculpture gallery.
Kristy Winter 2022.

"You like my human number two sculptures, huh? Where is this gallery you speak of?"

"It is down the street in a special pipe. Yours would be the first art sculptures we are inviting. We would bring many other dung beetle sellers to look at your sculptures. What do you say?"

"You want me to bring all of my sculptures I made?"

"Yes. We would love to have all of them."

"Alright, but you are going to need to be careful pulling them out."

"We would like you to have the honor of pulling them out. We have a special vehicle to move it in."

"Ok, I will move them, but I will need your help. I have 1,000 sculptures of human number two specimens."

"Alright, let's get to work."

They finished putting all of the human poop sculptures in the special vehicles and placed the two dung beetles in the front of the vehicle to ride in. Then the cockroach plumber put that into a special pocket that shrinks items so he could carry it out.

"Alright, ma'am. We have removed your clog in your toilet. You shouldn't have anymore problems with it."

"Oh, thank you so much! I don't know how you did it, but here's an extra $100 for all your hard work. I know it wasn't easy."

"You are welcome, ma'am. Have a nice day. Thank you for your business!"

"Goodbye and thanks again!"

The cockroach plumber took the dung beetles to the special pipe art gallery and they unloaded all of the human number two sculptures.

"Wow! That's some special vehicle you got. This place is great! So, when do the sellers come to see my art?"

"They are waiting outside this door we just have to let them in."

They let the 1,000 sellers in and all of the sculptures were bought.

"Alright, now I need some more samples, so I can make more."

"Yes, well we have a special room over here where your samples come right to you."

"Wow! Thank you so much!"

"We will have another showing as soon as you are done with the next ones. Just give us a call at 1-800-888-3213, and we'll send them right over."

"Wow! Thank you so much!"

"Goodbye. Hope to see you soon."

"Thanks again!"

"You're welcome."

The Aerobics Instructor.

"Yes, hello. I was wondering if you knew how to get rid of a caterpillar in my cat's litter box? The caterpillar keeps doing aerobics in her litter box and she can't concentrate to go number one or two."

"Hmm. We have not seen this problem before. Does your cat like aerobics?"

"I don't think so."

"Hmm. Hold on, someone just came in. Let me see if they have any suggestions."

"Ok."

"Alright, Catty Pillar I need your help. This lady on the phone says her cat can't poop or pee in her litter box when a caterpillar does aerobics. Do you know what to do?"

"Ahh. Yes, I know what to do."

"Ok. I'll tell her you're on your way, just let me get her address for you."

"Ok."

"Ma'am, may I have your address? I think I have someone who can solve your problem."

"I live at 2122 Litter Box Lane Cat, Kansas 66112."

"Alright, Catty Pillar will be right over."

"Thank you so much!"

Catty Pillar arrives at Kitty Box's house and knocks on the door. Kitty answers and takes Catty to the garage.

"See she can't concentrate with all that noise and distraction."

Caterpillar Aerobics
Kristy Winter 2022.
Stretch Right and squeeze!
High knees up and down.

"Yes, I see. Let me see what I can do."

Catty walks over to the caterpillar and talks to him.

"Hello, I am Catty Pillar. So nice to meet you. This cat can't seem to concentrate when you do your aerobics. Could we move you to another spot in here and make you a special gym?"

"No, thank you. I like the feel of these rocks just fine, but I would like it if she got her hair done every once in awhile it's pretty gross!"

"Oh, I see. Let me talk to her."

"Okay."

"Excuse me miss. Could I ask you a question?"

"Yes, what is it?"

"Ok. My new friend here would like you to get your hair done every once in awhile. Would that be ok?"

"Alright, but he has to do it and I want it in a cupcake shape, please."

"Alright, I'll tell him."

"Excuse me sir."

"Yes."

"She wants you to do her hair for her and in a cupcake shape, please."

"Finally, I thought she'd never ask. I will get my crew right away."

Cupcake, the cat, finally was able to go to the bathroom.

"Finally, peace and quiet."

"Alright, Cupcake you ready?"

"Yes, Bubble Gum. Make me look fabulous!"

Bubble Gum and his crew worked their magic and gave her the cupcake hair style she wanted.

"Oh, thank you so much!"

(Just wanted to thank Yue for her special picture she drew for me.)

"We promise to stop doing aerobics when you have to go, but you must let us do your hair once a week."

"Sounds good, Bubble Gum. It's a deal."

"Alright, ma'am. Problem solved. They are going to work it out."

"Oh, I forgot he and his crew did her hair. They got into a fight two weeks ago and stopped talking to each other. Thank you so much. Here's an extra $100 for your trouble."

"Your welcome, ma'am. No, trouble at all. Thank you and goodbye. Take care you two."

"We will. Thank you again."

"Hope your Kitty Hair Salon gets lots of business."

"Thanks."

Hello everyone, just wanted to thank all my special helpers who gave me lots of inspiration in writing this book. All of your thoughts and suggestions really meant a lot to me. This book was so much fun to do. I really love to draw insects and show you what they look like in real life. I also like to research them and add the scientific names to the story to make it more interesting. It was so much fun doing all the advertisements for the insects as well.

www.ingramcontent.com/pod-product-compliance
Lightning Source LLC
Chambersburg PA
CBHW081156130726
47996CB00009B/3146